Strength in Simplicity

Emmanuel de Gibergues

Strength in Simplicity

The Busy Catholic's Guide
to Growing Closer to God

SOPHIA INSTITUTE PRESS
Manchester, New Hampshire

Strength in Simplicity was published by Sophia Institute Press in 2000 under the title *Keep It Simple*. It is an abridged and slightly revised edition of *Simplicity According to the Gospel* (New York: P. J. Kenedy and Sons, c. 1914).

Cover design: Coronation Media in collaboration
with Perceptions Design Studio.

On the cover: "Holy Cross" (59374339)
© Hans Engbers / Shutterstock.com.

Sophia Institute Press
Box 5284, Manchester, NH 03108
1-800-888-9344
www.SophiaInstitute.com
Sophia Institute Press® is a registered trademark of Sophia Institute.

Nihil Obstat: F. Thomas Bergh, O.S.B., *Censor Deputatus*
Imprimatur: Edm. Can. Surmont, *Vicarius Generalis*
Westmonasterii, June 30, 1914

Library of Congress Cataloging-in-Publication Data

Gibergues, Emmanuel de, 1855-1919.
   [Keep it simple]
   Strength in simplicity : the busy Catholic's guide to growing closer to God / Emmanuel de Gibergues.
      pages cm
   Previously published under title: Keep it simple : the busy Catholic's guide to growing closer to God, c2000.
   ISBN 978-1-62282-218-8 (pbk. : alk. paper) 1. Spiritual life — Catholic Church. 2. Simplicity — Religious aspects — Catholic Church. 3. Catholic Church — Doctrines. I. Title.
   BX2350.2.G53 2014
   241'.4 — dc23

                  2014019291

First printing

Contents

Strength in Simplicity

Editor's note: The biblical references in the following pages are based on the Douay-Rheims translation of the Old and New Testaments. Where applicable, quotations have been cross-referenced with the differing names and enumeration in the Revised Standard Version, using the following symbol: (RSV =).

Chapter One

⌒

Understand what simplicity is

Why does the Gospel present to us the dove as the model and ideal of Christian simplicity, saying, "Be ye . . . simple as doves"?[1] To understand this, we must have a clear idea of what simplicity really is.

Simplicity, or purity of intention, consists in keeping before yourself, in all your thoughts, words, and acts, one and the same end, one and the same object — namely, the pleasing of God, or, more accurately, the doing of His will. Thus understood, simplicity appears to us as a virtue at once essential and far-reaching.

"Man was created for God," says St. Ignatius[2] at the beginning of his *Spiritual Exercises*, in that first meditation, which he justly calls *fundamental*, because it is the

---

[1] Matt. 10:16.

[2] St. Ignatius of Loyola (c. 1491-1556), founder of the Jesuit Order.

foundation of the whole Christian order. These admirable *Spiritual Exercises* are based entirely upon this first profound truth; they are, as it were, its commentary and development.

God is, in effect, the sole veritable end, the last end, of man. If man sees only God, seeks only God, and attaches himself only to God; if he voluntarily directs his thoughts, his words, his acts, and his whole life toward God; if, in some sort, he passes amid creatures without pausing, if he fails to find in them his repose as in an end, but desires to rest only in God — then he is in the way of truth and order; he is righteous and holy, because he is perfectly simple. The catechism expresses the same idea in saying, "Man is created to know God, to love Him, and to serve Him, and thus to reach eternal life."

Now, how do we refer our thoughts, words, and actions to God? By our *intention* — that is, by the *motive* that determines our will to produce them freely. Our operations and our actions considered in themselves, independent of the motive that has prompted them, have, properly speaking, no moral value; they are bodies without souls. The moral value is *in us*, in our free will, which is the soul of all that we do and gives to our actions their meaning and their worth.

Men judge us according to the exterior, according to the words that they hear and the actions that they see. This is why they are so often unjust, severe, and ill-natured. But God judges us according to what He sees within; He looks on our heart, our will, our motive, and our intention, and it is according to these that He approves or blames, rewards or punishes.

Such is the meaning of these words in the Gospel: "If thy eye be single, thy whole body shall be lightsome. But if thy eye be evil, thy whole body shall be darksome."[3] The eye signifies the intention, for, just as the eye directs our steps, so does the intention guide the movements of our soul. The intention is the eye of our soul. If our soul looks toward God, if it freely directs toward Him our thoughts, words, and actions, then all that we do, all that we say, and all that we think becomes by this very fact supernatural and good. The Gospel expresses this in saying, "Thy whole body shall be lightsome."

Thus, the merit of human actions lies wholly in the intention. Our actions have simply the value of our intention.

[3] Matt. 6:22-23.

Thenceforth, simplicity becomes the *soul of the spiritual life*, since it consists precisely in purity of intention. Simplicity gives to the life of the spirit all its depth and value. The simple soul is ever pleasing to God, because it ever looks toward Him, and seeks for Him always, having no ambition other than to do His will in order to procure His glory.

To be simple is to see, love, and desire God in all creatures and in all things; it is to unify one's life with God.

Chapter Two

Learn to perfect your simplicity

There are degrees in simplicity. Simplicity becomes more elevated and perfect as the intention is more effectively present and as the intention is more pure.

Simplicity asks that we exclude from our intentions all that would be contrary to the divine will and, above all, incompatible with the possession of God, who is our last end — in a word, all that theology calls *sin*, mortal or venial.

In the case of an end permitted or even commanded by God, but which is secondary, simplicity asks that we not attach ourselves to it as to a final end, nor incline ourselves toward an earthly good, be it ever so legitimate, with a desire and a love that would cause us to prefer it to an eternal good.

But, apart from these exceptions, simplicity permits us all freedom concerning inferior and secondary ends when they are legitimate; for example, to express our respect and love for our parents, our gratitude to our benefactors, or our compassion for those who suffer. It permits us to take measures to improve our health, to succeed in an examination, to advance in a career, and to obtain lawful advantages. This is, indeed, all permitted, often praiseworthy, and sometimes commanded.

All these intentions are in the right order of things, because they are conformable to the will of God. In pursuing them, it is God whom we are seeking, and it is God whom we please, if we are careful to refer all to Him.

Therefore, if we firmly determine to exclude all that is displeasing to God, to seek as a secondary end solely what He permits or commands, to attach ourselves only to Him as our final end — in other words, if, being in a state of grace, we generously accept all the obligations of a Christian life, having the sincere desire to offer all to God — our intention is pure. We effectively practice simplicity as long as our soul remains in this state and attitude, even if we are not always actually thinking of it. "The traveler who is on the right road," says St. Thomas,[4] "has no need to think at each step of his destination."

---

[4] St. Thomas Aquinas (c. 1225-1274), Dominican philosopher and theologian.

In like manner, the soul that has the explicit and unchanging determination of reaching God need not renew its intention for every act accomplished. So long as the first intention has not been retracted, the intention virtually remains, according to the theologians, which means that by its virtue and its own force, it enters into all our actions, penetrates them, and communicates its value to them. By reason of a definite and persevering intention, the soul attains its end; it journeys to God, as a river in its course flows to the sea.

If we decide to act in all things for God, if we do not retract this first determination, if it has any influence whatsoever upon our actions, although we may not be actually conscious of it, we are on the right road; we approach our last end; we work for God; we already possess, in a certain degree at least, simplicity and purity of intention.

Nevertheless, if during our actions we often think of God, to offer all to Him; if we often revive in our hearts the desire to love Him and to please Him; if we renew at the moment our determination to refer all to Him — it is obvious that the strength and intensity of our intention is thereby increased, and the merit of our acts becomes accordingly greater. The more our intention is present and intense, the holier our actions are, because they are inspired by a greater simplicity.

In like manner, the motives that enter into the original intention to act for God have in themselves, and give to the intention and to the act, a most unequal value. Thus, you can have in view the acquisition of legitimate temporal blessings and, to this end, may offer alms, prayers, and sacrifices. This intention is praiseworthy, if accompanied by true submission to the will of God. But it is the least perfect of all, because its object does not go beyond this world. You are at the lowest degree of simplicity, because your motive, although legitimate, is the least lofty of all.

You can act from fear of the punishments of God. If it were a cowardly fear, it would corrupt all. If you were to avoid sin only from fear of the punishment, in such a way as to wish that the punishment did not exist, in order that you might freely commit the sin, your intention would be evil and to be condemned. But if your fear is filial, if you admit the propriety of God's punishment, if you avoid sin from fear of losing God, your intention is good. It is praised and commended by Scripture.[5] You

---

[5] Cf. Ps. 110:10 (RSV = Ps. 111:10); Prov. 1:7.

have already attained to a motive superior to the preceding one; it is no longer temporal blessings that you covet, but spiritual blessings that you fear to lose.

If, further, you regard these spiritual blessings with the desire to gain the promised reward, if you say with the psalmist, "I have inclined my heart to do Thy justifications forever for the reward,"[6] your intention rises higher and becomes better. It is already noble and very holy, for the reward promised to the righteous is God Himself, according to the promise given to Abram: "I will be thy reward exceedingly great."[7]

Finally, you can act directly for God. Of all intentions, this is obviously the most perfect. Moreover, this intention may be formulated in two fashions.

You can, in the first place, purpose to please God, and so to merit His favors and benefits. Indeed, to act thus is to already love God, to love Him greatly and above all else.

There exists, however, an intention that is loftier, purer, because there exists a love that is more perfect. You can love God for Himself alone, without the slightest

[6] Ps. 118:112 (RSV = Ps. 119:112).
[7] Cf. Gen. 15:1.

thought of self, without any touch of egoism. You can forget yourself, "lose your life,"[8] as the Gospel says, in order to see only God.

It is no question of suppressing the virtue of hope to the advantage of charity; we would fall into an error condemned by the Church. We must desire God, seek Him, and hope for Him. And in reality, whether conscious of it or not, the soul hopes all the more as its love is greater.

Nevertheless, when the soul feels a great love for God, the moment comes when it forgets His gifts in contemplation of the divine Giver. The soul loves for the sake of loving and serves for the sake of serving, heedless of the joy and blessings that such love and service will bring it. "This act of love," says Msgr. Gay, "doubtless belongs to the soul which makes it, but it no longer has any place therein. God alone is all."[9] It is thus that the saints have loved God; and it is because their love went to such lengths that they were saints. Such generous impulses, divine oblivion, and total self-abnegation,

---

[8] Cf. Matt. 10:39.

[9] *"Pureté d'Intention," Instructions pour les Personnes du Monde*, Vol. 2, ch. 5.

such raptures of the heart and transports of pure love, are ever to be found in their lives and in their works.

David cried, "For what have I in Heaven? And besides Thee, what do I desire upon earth?"[10] St. Bernard wrote, "Pure love is not mercenary; it does not find its strength in hope; it is content to love."[11] St. Thomas asked of God no other reward than God Himself.

St. John of the Cross went so far as to say, "The true lover, even if he thought it possible that his good works might escape the eye of God, and pass unrewarded, would love God no less in consequence, and would do no less for Him."[12] And elsewhere, "It is the property of perfect love to be unconcerned with self, neither to desire nor reserve aught for self, and to claim nothing for self, but to give all to the Beloved."[13]

Such was the unchanging love of Mary; the eye of God never found within her heart the slightest shadow of self-interest or of vanity.

[10] Ps. 72:25 (RSV = Ps. 73:25).

[11] St. Bernard (1090-1153; Abbot of Clairvaux), Sermon 83, "On the Canticles."

[12] St. John of the Cross (1542-1591; mystic and joint founder of the Discalced Carmelites), Sentences.

[13] "Explanation of the Canticle," strophe 32.

Strength in Simplicity

Such, above all, was the love of Jesus for His Father. "Christ did not please Himself,"[14] says St. Paul, but always regarded the divine will; He never for one instant turned His attention therefrom and could in truth say, "I do always the things that please my Father."[15]

Thus, there are degrees in simplicity and purity of intention, as there are degrees in love. As the intention is purer and more present — that is to say, as it turns directly and vigorously toward God, freeing itself from all other motives — the love becomes purer and more perfect, and the act accomplished becomes holier and more meritorious. Perfect simplicity, perfect purity of intention, therefore, constitutes in effect the purest and most perfect love.

[14] Rom. 15:3.
[15] Cf. John 8:29.

Chapter Three

Discover simplicity's fruits

A virtue so enhanced, of such value, which is the quintessence of Scripture and of the Gospel, and the very spirit of the religion taught by Christ, cannot fail to be fruitful. And truly the fruits of simplicity are marvelous. The Gospel sums them up when it says, "If thy eye be single, thy whole body shall be lightsome. But if thy eye be evil, thy whole body shall be darksome."[16]

These words give us two precious and very practical maxims.

In the first place, without simplicity, at least in a certain degree, it is impossible to please God; for although men see that which appears outwardly, God looks at the heart — namely, the intention that prompts our actions. If you are a slave to public opinion, prejudice, and human respect; if you allow yourself to be led by a word, a

[16] Matt. 6:22-23.

glance, or a smile; if you act for the world — you cannot please God; you are no longer a Christian. "If I yet pleased men," says St. Paul, "I would not be the servant of Christ."[17]

Even that which is good in itself could not please God without simplicity. "Take heed that you do not your justice before men, to be seen by them; otherwise you shall not have a reward of your Father who is in Heaven."[18] In the same way, if you act from egotistical motives, self-love, vain complacency, and personal satisfaction — if, in a word, you take the credit for the good that you do or the virtues you practice — their intrinsic value is lost in God's sight. "You put all into a bag with holes."[19]

You may multiply your prayers, make the longest meditations, and the most frequent Communions; "you may," as the apostle says, "have the gift of prophecy, and know all mysteries and all knowledge; you may give all your goods to the poor, and your body to be burned," and by your charitable works merit the admiration of

[17] Cf. Gal. 1:10.
[18] Matt. 6:1.
[19] Agg. 1:6 (RSV = Hag. 1:6).

the whole world; and yet, if you do all this for yourself, if your intention is a wholly selfish one, "if you have not charity, which alone renders the intention pure, [then] all that will profit you nothing."[20] All is lost before God, and worthless for your salvation. Your eye is not single; your body cannot be lightsome.

And what is more, if no action can please God unless it is referred to Him in all simplicity, an action even good in itself becomes evil when the intention is evil: "If thy eye be evil, thy whole body shall be darksome."

The Gospel charges us, it is true, "Let your light shine before men, that they may see your good works," but it immediately adds, "that they may glorify your Father who is in Heaven."[21] We should edify our neighbor by our words, acts, and works, but we must not seek to gratify our vanity thereby. "Our intention," says St. Gregory, "should remain hidden."[22]

We must refer all to God and to His glory, and not to our own. If we seek our own glory and not that of God,

---

[20] Cf. 1 Cor. 13:2-3.

[21] Matt. 5:16.

[22] St. Gregory the Great (c. 540-604; Pope from 590), *The Gospel of St. Matthew*, Homily 11, sect. 7, ch. 13.

even good becomes evil in God's sight. St. Vincent de Paul[23] expresses this in the following words: "It would be better to be cast, bound hand and foot, upon red-hot coals, than to do a good work from vanity."

On the contrary, by means of simplicity, all becomes clear, all is transformed, all becomes profitable and good, and all is pleasing in God's sight.

If the thought of duty inspires you, if you have in view the good of souls and the glory of God, if you sincerely seek the will of your Father who is in Heaven, then all that you do takes on a supernatural value. "If the root is holy," says the apostle, "so are the branches."[24] The duties of your position, your pious exercises, your good works, your family relations, your sorrows, your joys, your trials, your sufferings, your loneliness, your forced inactivity — all, in a word, without exception, becomes holy and agreeable to God by the purity of intention.

If the eye is single — that is to say, without defect or blemish of any kind; if it is healthy; if the light penetrates it and illumines the whole body and its every

---

[23] St. Vincent de Paul (c. 1580-1660), founder of the Lazarist Fathers and the Sisters of Charity.

[24] Rom. 11:16.

movement. Likewise, if your soul is simple — that is to say, healthy — the divine light penetrates it. You see God, you comprehend Him, you do all in Him and for Him, and all your thoughts, words, and acts become good and holy.

O admirable fruits of simplicity! O marvelous effects of a pure intention! Things have no longer any value of their own; they take their value from the intention that inspires them. The widow's mite mentioned in the Gospel weighs more in God's sight than the vast sums given by the rich,[25] and a glass of water given in the name of Jesus Christ is the price of eternity.[26]

"What, then, does it matter," says St. Augustine,[27] "if your purse is small? You can give much with your heart and will by doing nothing save for God's good pleasure."

Even the most ordinary and most material act may become spiritual and holy: "Therefore, whether you eat or drink, or whatsoever else you do, do all for the glory of God."[28]

---

[25] Mark 12:41-43.

[26] Cf. Matt. 10:42.

[27] St. Augustine (354-430), Bishop of Hippo.

[28] 1 Cor. 10:31.

Finally, the intention has of itself such a value in the eyes of God that the desire alone, if sincere and true, is accounted as the act. Suppose I have the firm intention to carry out a work of charity, but am prevented by circumstances beyond my control; if it had depended upon me, I would have accomplished it. My intention before God has the same value as the work itself. Hence the extreme importance in the spiritual life of holy desires, and the unthinkable riches to which they can lead.

St. Mary Magdalene de' Pazzi relates how, in a vision, St. Aloysius Gonzaga appeared in wondrous glory.[29] And amazed that a saint who died so young could have acquired so high a degree of merit, God revealed to her that this exceptional glory was due to the intensity and ardor of his desires — which is to say, the simplicity and purity of his intentions.

It is by simplicity that the righteous man, "being made perfect in a short space, fulfills a long time,"[30] because he lives uniquely for God and seeks only to please Him. Simplicity makes of our life one continual homage

[29] St. Mary Magdalene de' Pazzi (1566-1607), Carmelite mystic; St. Aloysius Gonzaga (1568-1591), patron saint of youth.

[30] Wisd. 4:13.

to God; it supernaturalizes and sanctifies our works, words, and thoughts, our most secret desires, and the slightest movements of our heart.

And simplicity produces still other admirable effects. It gives to the soul those two excellent qualities which St. Teresa[31] declared indispensable to beginners in the spiritual life — namely, joy and liberty of spirit.

The most generous person, if not simple, is troubled, anxious, and endlessly discouraged. His very generosity sometimes inclines him to be scrupulous and, under pretext of delicacy, warps his conscience. "Am I not deceived?" he cries. "Has God forgiven me? Should I in truth do this? Am I on the right path?" He is continually asking himself a thousand disturbing and confusing questions. By self-introspection, he ends by losing his clearness of vision. He inevitably falls into a profound melancholy, a fatal discouragement.

The simple soul escapes all such dangers because he looks to God far more than to creatures and places himself above all that obscures, fatigues, and exasperates the soul who is not simple.

---

[31] Possibly St. Teresa of Avila (1515-1582), Carmelite nun and mystic. — ED.

Strength in Simplicity

The soul who is not simple is represented in the Gospel by Martha, who was restless, anxious, and concerned with many things. The simple soul is represented by Mary, tranquilly seated at the feet of the Master, drinking in each word and solely mindful of His pleasure. The simple soul has found "the better part," "the one thing necessary";[32] he is wholly given to God.

Without self-preoccupation, without artifice or hypocrisy, without subterfuge or dissimulation, without fear of the world's opinion, speaking as he thinks, his heart in one sense on his sleeve, such a person is always calm and tranquil. He goes on his way unanxious and untroubled, his spirit free, and his heart full of joy and peace. Neither lack of success, contempt, gossip, trials, nor even his own falls, sins, and imperfections — nothing in this world — can disturb him. He has found the peace that Jesus gives, "the joy that none can take away."[33]

Simplicity frees the soul from the burden, sometimes crushing, of the things of this world; it delivers the soul from the many vain anxieties so hard to bear. It makes it light, free, and joyous.

[32] Cf. Luke 10:42.
[33] Cf. John 16:22.

And, further, simplicity produces sincerity and utterly destroys the evil that is perhaps most to be dreaded for the soul's progress — namely, illusion. Father Faber, that profound psychologist, in a spiritual conference on illusions, after having shown the extent of the harm they do in the domain of spiritual life, declares that simplicity is the only remedy for this terrible and universal evil. The souls who examine themselves most closely are not those who know themselves the best, nor, above all, those who correct themselves most quickly. By unbandaging a wound to see whether it has healed, you end by aggravating it. On the contrary, the soul who looks to God rapidly learns self-knowledge and, what is much more important, detachment.

God is truth, and by contemplating Him, the soul becomes like Him. The simple soul knows itself at a glance; and if it happens that in certain hours of fatigue or forgetfulness the soul touches earth, no sooner is it conscious of this than up it rises by a stroke of the wing and soars rapidly away to the highest regions, from which a moment's carelessness had caused its fall.

The simple soul knows itself because it knows God, who is pure light and who enlightens the conscience. Such a soul recognizes its wretchedness and flees from itself, in proportion as it seeks God and loves Him. The simple soul, being sincere, is also *generous* in the effort to overcome itself.

The majority of your faults come from a lack of simplicity. When you are given over to envy and jealousy, when you are agitated, tortured, sometimes by violent desires or human affections of too absorbing a nature, you are the reverse of simple, for you look only to the creature, and the simple soul sees only God.

Simplicity makes the soul generous; it unifies the soul's operations, strengthens its courage, and revives its ardor. It prompts the soul to the noblest enterprises and keeps it from all fatigue. Like the dove, seemingly effortless in its flight through space, the simple soul is troubled by nothing. God bears the soul up and accomplishes in it the great things that it does: "He that is mighty has done great things for me."[34]

Simplicity edifies your neighbor, for it is the source of a sweet nature, serenity, kindness, affability, and all those lovable and attractive virtues which charm, repose, inspire confidence, and do real good. In the soul that lacks simplicity, there is always something egotistical and

[34] Luke 1:49.

selfish that comes out in the person's attitude and bearing, his manners, words, and actions.

The simple are disconcerting in their humility and self-forgetfulness. They make us feel God and touch Him. Beside them one is safe; one cannot approach or see them without being the better for it. They little suspect the good they do, or they find it most surprising. And the more unconscious they are, the more good is done, accordingly as there is less of self and more of God. All their actions are blessed, because they are done in the spirit of God and for love of Him.

Finally, we could never tell the joy they give to God and the glory they procure for Him. At each instant of the day, they sanctify the name of God and extend His reign, because at each instant they do His will. Even their rest and sleep become a hymn to the praise of the Most High, for they sleep, but their heart watches,"[35] always by the persevering purity of their intention.

Spotless doves, they unceasingly ravish the heart of their divine Spouse; and it is in Him, in the sacred wounds received for love of us, that they take up their abode and find their rest after the day's long flight.

[35] Cf. Cant. 5:2 (RSV = Song of Sol. 5:2).

Chapter Four

*Recognize the signs
of simplicity*

How can you tell whether you have acquired the virtue of simplicity? By four principal signs.

The first is *indifference to your own success*. When you do not succeed in an undertaking, whether it concerns your family, the education and future of your children, your duties toward your spouse, the management of your house, or be it something abroad, touching family connections, almsgiving, visits to the poor, or perhaps a conversion, what is it that troubles and discourages you? It is the failure to achieve the sought-for end — a legitimate end doubtless, but human. You have had in view the result, the success, the work in itself. You have failed in purity of intention.

It is plain, indeed, that if your intention had been pure, if you had sought before all the goodwill and pleasure of God, you would say to yourself, "Since God has not willed this result, neither will I. Moreover, if I have acted for God, if I have sought to please Him, I most certainly have succeeded, and God must be content, for I have done what I could, all in my power. Therefore, I should be satisfied and as calm as if success had crowned my efforts."

The second sign is *joy in the success of others or in their spiritual progress*. If your intention is straightforward and pure, you must desire all that honors, rejoices, and glorifies God. If those around you do good, and more than you do; if, in the same work, another is more successful than you; if a work of the same sort as yours is more prosperous than your own, or prospers at the expense of yours, you should feel neither offense, nor jealousy, nor bitterness, nor sorrow, but should sincerely rejoice from the bottom of your heart, since God is thereby glorified.

Those who are exclusive, who think only of their own works, and of their own part therein, and who, with ill-disguised vexation, find everywhere competitors and rivals whom they would like to banish or eclipse are certainly lacking in purity of intention. In the same way, if the sight of another who, by effort, improves and becomes better annoys and irritates you — I am not speaking of a noble and holy emulation, which is legitimate and good — but if something in you would prevent this progress which is vexing to you, then you are lacking in purity of intention.

Purity of intention may be recognized by the sincere and veritable joy that we feel — or at least that we *freely wish* to feel by scorning any adverse feeling — at the thought of another's progress, or in view of the good that we see him accomplish.

The third sign of purity of intention is *attachment to the will of God,* that is, freedom from all willful preference for any one thing, from all decided attachment to anything. You may have inclinations either of nature or of grace. You may feel spontaneously attracted to this or to that. Certain are more drawn toward an interior life, others to an active life; some to visit the poor, others to nurse the sick or to instruct children or those who are uneducated. But you should be prepared, if necessary, to sacrifice your personal tastes readily, to give yourself up to whatever obedience exacts of you. You should so uniquely attach yourself to the will of God that, once clearly manifested, you will be ready to accept it generously, in spite of all reluctance and the necessary sacrifice of your own inclinations.

The fourth sign is *neither to desire nor to court the praise and approbation of men for the good that you do,* and to retain your calm and interior peace if you receive only reproaches and blame. You must say to yourself, "If I have done my duty and accomplished the will of God, it is all that I desired; nothing else matters to me."

If you do not find in your heart these four signs of purity of intention, if one alone is lacking, or if you find them incomplete or imperfect, it proves that your intentions are not wholly pure and that there is some flaw in your simplicity, or that perhaps you are entirely lacking in this virtue.

You must strive to acquire it, daily to advance in it. And in order that it may bear all its fruits, and that most abundantly, strive to acquire it in the highest degree and in the fullness of its perfection.

You should have the heart of that woman of whom St. Liguori[36] speaks: a Dominican on pilgrimage with St. Louis found her in Palestine, holding in one hand a vase filled with water and in the other a burning torch. Asked by the friar their meaning, she replied, "With this water I would extinguish the fires of Hell, and with this torch I would destroy the heavens, that henceforth

---

[36] St. Alphonsus Liguori (1696-1787), moral theologian and founder of the Redemptorists.

God might no longer be served from fear of Hell, or hope of Heaven, but solely for love."

You should forever exclaim with St. Bernard, "May I love Thee, Lord, for Thyself alone! Not for the happiness of loving Thee, but solely to do Thy good pleasure, and to content Thy heart!"

You should be able to say with the divine Master: "I seek not my own will, but the will of Him that sent me; for I do always the things that please Him."[37]

Then only will you have perfect simplicity.

[37] John 8:29.

Chapter Five

☙

Practice simplicity toward God

Let us now enter into detail and, in some sort, draw the portrait of simplicity covering the vast field wherein you are called to exercise it.

Simplicity is the perfection of your relation to God. "Walk before me, and be perfect,"[38] said God to Abram. The simple soul follows this divine counsel and carries out this admirable program. He walks before God; he is conscious of His presence. He ever sees Him. He has but one desire: that of pleasing God. He understands the exceptional importance of pious exercises; he clings to them for no sensible attraction — ever liable to come and go — but by the free effort of a resolute and persevering will. He does not seek therein his own satisfaction, rest, or immediate reward, as would a hireling. He seeks only God's will and glory.

[38] Gen. 17:1.

If he finds sensible consolation, sweetness, and joy, far from rejecting such favors, he receives them with gratitude for God's goodness; but he does not rest in them with complacency, nor count upon them. He loves God more than all His gifts, and instead of attributing these divine graces to him, he turns all to the glory of God.

The simple soul is more apt in contemplation than in meditation. Before a work of art, a marvelous picture, you forget yourself. You are absorbed by what you see; in an instant, all the faculties of your soul are ravished, and in a way suspended, until, finally, you come back to earth. The simple soul never tires of admiring the eternal and infinite beauty. Sometimes he sees it in God Himself, and sometimes in the humanity of Christ, as in a spotless mirror. He never argues and seldom reasons; he looks, contemplates, and escapes from self to be absorbed and lost in God.[39]

---

[39] "The soul must be ever steadfast in prayer," says St. Francis de Sales, "and permitted neither to note what he does, nor to find satisfaction therein. Alas, our satisfactions and consolations, far from pleasing God, only satisfy our own miserable self-love. He who is very careful lovingly to please Jesus Christ has neither heart nor time to turn toward self; his spirit ever tends where love carries it" (*Entretien* XIII).

In the case of the saints, this goes to the length of transports and ecstasies. Borne away on simplicity's powerful wings, they penetrate to the very heart of the Divinity. Thus, the prophet Daniel was seized, ravished, and overcome because, says Scripture, he was "a man of desires,"[40] that is to say, a man wholly simple, desiring only God.

If the simple soul finds in prayer only dryness, if he is as "in a desert land, where there is no way and no water,"[41] he is not discouraged. He sees the will of God in these grievous trials and loses nothing of his calm and peace.

If the duties of his state or unforeseen circumstances, if charity or illness — something, in a word, that is willed by God — prevents him from applying himself to his customary pious exercises and obliges him even to discontinue his Communions, he is neither troubled nor discouraged. He recalls our Lord's reply to Père Alverez, who, overwhelmed with occupations, complained that he had no time for prayer: "When I no longer abide with you, let it suffice that I make use of you."

[40] Dan. 9:23.
[41] Ps. 62:3 (RSV = Ps. 63:1).

Strength in Simplicity

The simple soul is admirable in his faith and piety toward the Church, the Sacraments, and all things holy. His faith cannot be shaken. Save by the express will of God, who sanctifies the most holy souls by trying them, doubt is unknown to him. His faith is clear and cloudless, pure and upright. His submission to all the teachings of the Church is ready, joyous, filial, and complete.

In the confessional, he sees God in the priest. He confesses his sins without agitation, confusion, or reservation. He says neither more nor less, neither too much nor too little; he says that which is, and as it is. He speaks to Jesus, and it is He whom he hears; he is yielding and ready to learn, perfectly humble and obedient. During the absolution, he sees the blood of Jesus flowing over him; he is filled with contrition, gratitude, and love. He emerges from this saving flood renewed with more strength to overcome himself, more devotion in the service of others.

During Mass, the simple soul is on Calvary, at the foot of the Cross. He sees Jesus raise His bleeding arms toward His Father — Jesus, who pardons, blesses, and prays, who suffers, and who dies. When he receives Communion, the whole of Heaven comes down into his heart. He is overwhelmed with joy and happiness.

He is wholly absorbed by the marvels that take place within him. It is with a mighty effort that he tears himself from his thanksgiving after Communion. He is all inflamed, consumed by the fires of divine love.

Grace works in this soul without opposition the most wonderful transformations. The person ever advances in virtue before God and man. He is "the sweet odor of Christ"[42] to those who come near him. Seeking God alone in the Sacraments and the Church, he finds Him therein, and in superabundance.

[42] Cf. 2 Cor. 2:15.

Chapter Six

Practice simplicity
toward yourself

With relation to himself, the simple soul is both sincere and courageous. He is not forever multiplying his examinations of conscience, nor looking into his own heart, but his glance is penetrating, rapid, and profound.

His conscience is without secrets, hidden corners, darkness, or even shadow. All is in a bright light — the light of God. He has no need of lengthy self-analysis, nor a need to argue with himself; a hasty survey shows him what he is. Without often regarding himself, he knows himself perfectly and, what is far better, corrects himself.

Many seek contrition in the consideration of their faults and the ugliness of sin and its consequences. The simple soul draws contrition chiefly from the contemplation of God, in the view of his own offenses against the Divine Majesty and the sorrow he has caused to the heart of God.

Strength in Simplicity

When Peter had denied his Master, a glance from Jesus pierced his heart through, and drew therefrom an inexhaustible source of tears.[43] The simple soul looks at Jesus, and Jesus looks at him, and His glance, like a fiery arrow, penetrates him with sorrow and repentance. His contrition is higher and more perfect because it is inspired by pure love.

Also, his generosity is incredible, and his progress marvelous. As fire melts ice and consumes straw, as the sun instantaneously dispels the heaviest mist and shows forth the blue depths of a cloudless sky, so does simplicity dispel indifference and tepidity, so does it destroy sin and curb all unruly inclinations with prodigious ease and promptitude, because simplicity is the practice and the very act of pure love.

After freeing himself from sin, the simple soul mounts rapidly toward God, as the dove with a vigorous stroke of the wing at once soars away to the loftiest regions.

The simple soul retains his simplicity even in his *desire* for perfection. There are generous souls who passionately long for perfection and ardently endeavor to attain it. But the ever-watchful enemy is there and,

---

[43] Luke 22:61-62.

unable to tempt them by evil means, tempts them, as St. Ignatius points out, "under the appearance of good." To this desire for perfection, you bring too great an eagerness, a restlessness and agitation in which there is something of self. You desire perfection for itself or for yourself more than for God, and the self-love that enters into this effort of the soul corrupts its purity, and by so much diminishes its value.

Be simple, therefore, in your desire for perfection. "Rise not till you have rested,"[44] says Scripture, which is to say, do not be in too great a hurry. "Don't outdistance Providence," St. Vincent de Paul used to say. You must desire perfection only in the measure that God wills it for you.

"Spiritual lovers, spouses of the Celestial King," says St. Francis de Sales, "do not purify themselves to be pure, nor do they adorn themselves to be beautiful, but solely to please their Celestial Spouse. Their confidence in His goodness relieves them of all eagerness and mistrust of not being sufficiently beautiful, and makes them content with a quiet, faithful, and conscientious preparation."

[44] Cf. Ps. 126:2 (RSV = Ps. 127:2).

Nevertheless, do not limit the intensity of your desires, provided that you keep them always wholly subject to God's good pleasure. St. Teresa encouraged her nuns to carry their desires of perfection to the highest possible degree, and God incites us all to this.

And, furthermore, you must desire to reach perfection, not according to the ways and means suggested by your scanty wisdom, nor according to your own designs and plans, but always and in all things according to the adorable designs of the Eternal Wisdom and the inscrutable way of the Infinite Goodness. In a word, never seek to follow your own lights in these labyrinths, where all human science goes astray, but, by an act of total self-abnegation, "rest your heart in the Lord," and, as the Gospel says, "lose your life to save it."[45] This is the fullest expression of simplicity.

Simplicity unites us so fully in all things to the will of God that it realizes the prayer of our Lord at the Last Supper: "My Father . . . may they be one as we also are one: I in them and Thou in me, that they may be made perfect in one."[46]

---

[45] Cf. Luke 17:33.
[46] Cf. John 17:22-23.

Chapter Seven

*Practice simplicity
in the world*

In the world, simplicity is the distinguishing mark of a true Christian, for the spirit of the world is, in effect, a spirit of duplicity and falsehood.

What falsehood and duplicity we find in appearances! Beneath a courteous and pleasing exterior, what meanness, vulgarity, and baseness often lurk. Each dissembles and disguises his true self, and all wear a mask in order to appear other than they are. What perpetual contradiction beneath the smiling words and the feelings of their hearts! They flatter out of vanity and praise from self-interest those to whom they look for certain advantages; whereas in reality they are jealous, and despise and detest them. They dishonor the sacred terms of *affection* and *love*, using them to cloak the most dangerous liberties, contemptible vanities, and abject pleasures.

That world which Jesus Christ condemns, saying that it is "altogether evil," and for which He "could not pray,"[47] is diametrically opposed to simplicity. Every eccentricity, defect, and hypocrisy are to be found in it.

Indeed, we might say of certain assemblies that they are made up of a strange collection of birds: of peacocks, who strut about so that they may be admired; of parrots, who senselessly repeat at random what they have heard; of magpies, who chatter and annoy by torrents of piercing, spiteful words; of vultures, who devour the honor and reputation of their neighbor; of ravens, who thrive on all that is shameful; of ducks and hens, who puff and blow and patter about in the vulgarity of the commonplace — in short, of every sort of bird symbolic of depravity, baseness, and sin.

Only the dove, the simplicity of the Gospel, is absent, or at least to be found only in the person of the true Christian. And what a contrast he is to his surroundings — how restful, how beneficent! He who is simple has a fund of seriousness and earnestness that keeps him from talking thoughtlessly and from talking too much. He neither gossips, flatters, slanders, deceives, nor poses. He appears what he is, and he speaks as he thinks. He is always kind and charitable at heart, because he sees his

[47] Cf. John 17:9, 15.

neighbor in God and God in his neighbor. He never speaks ill of others, because he never thinks ill of them. He is neither indifferent nor unfeeling regarding the interests of those around him; on the contrary, he loves them with all his heart, because God commands it.

Now, in the love of the unsimple soul for his neighbor, there is a large proportion of self-interest, whereas he who is simple loves his neighbor for his neighbor's sake more than for his own satisfaction, and loves him still further for God. He loves as God loves, which means that his love is most pure and perfect. He has a horror of sin, but, like our Lord, he feels neither contempt nor aversion for the sinner. He is full of indulgence and kindness for all, without ever seeming to encourage or approve of evil and evildoers.

Subject like all of us to temptation, the simple person does not consent, but combats and subdues within himself that which he keeps from appearing without. He is simple, because his words come from his heart. Purity reigns in his conversation, as in his bearing and in his manner of dress, always natural and genuine, because his sentiments are just and charitable, being the sentiments of God, upon whom he models himself in all things.

Finally, he can be trusted to keep a secret; he is discretion itself without ceasing to be simple, because discretion could never be an enemy to truth. Thus we see reserve and sincerity, humility, purity, charity, amiability, kindness, and goodness all naturally thrive in the soul who is simple.

Then, again, he inspires an absolute confidence. All are drawn, irresistibly impelled, toward him. Simplicity gives him a moral ascendancy and an authority that he ever uses for good. He who is simple is as correct and modest in person and dress as the worldly person is the contrary. There is a reflection of God on his brow, in his eyes, and in his whole bearing.

As he looks at God, so God looks at him and "makes the light of His countenance to shine upon him."[48] He is beautiful with a beauty not of this world; simplicity is his sole adornment.

If you are simple, you will fear earthly beauty as a peril for you, a danger for others, a device and snare of Satan, an instrument of sin and perdition. If you are simple, you will ardently long for a different beauty beside which all the united beauties of this earth are as

[48] Cf. Ps. 4:7 (RSV = Ps. 4:6).

less than nothing. This superior beauty is born of virtue and the presence of God in a soul, His reflection on a countenance. It is made up of humility and sweetness, kindness and goodness, modesty and grace, charity and self-forgetfulness. It makes you like unto Christ, inspires respect and confidence, banishes all thought of evil, and attracts and charms in order to raise all up to God.

Chapter Eight

~

Practice simplicity
in all things

Simplicity will illumine and transform everything in your sight, making you see all in the light of God. It will show you the true end of life in the "one thing necessary"[49] of the Gospel, and will detach you from pleasure, success, riches, and all the vanities of this world. It will show you sin as the enemy of God, the irreconcilable adversary of Jesus Christ, the only evil to be feared. But it will take from your heart all hatred of the Church's persecutors; it will fill you with compassion for them. It will make you see in them creatures whose misfortune is even greater than their guilt — blind, lost souls on the road to Hell and deserving of all pity.[50]

[49] Luke 10:42.

[50] "If," said God to St. Catherine of Siena, "you witness an undeniable sin, you must separate the rose from its thorns, offering the sinner to me with a holy and fraternal compassion."

Strength in Simplicity

Simplicity will make you most careful to avoid all occasions of sin. Mistrustful of yourself, but confident in the all-powerful protection of God, you will be safe in the midst of even the most overwhelming temptations. Simplicity will be for you the ivory tower from within whose safe shelter you may defy the attacks of the enemy. "He who walks in simplicity walks in perfect safety."[51]

Simplicity will help you marvelously in suffering. You will no longer find it a crushing burden, an irritating, depleting wound, or an insurmountable obstacle to perfection. If you are simple, you will see suffering in the light of God's love and goodness. You will see in it, as it were, a mysterious remedy that God in His infinite love has chosen to make use of to wipe out and destroy your sins, to fill your heart with supernatural riches, to unite you more closely to Jesus Christ, so that you may cooperate with Him in the redemption of the world.

Simplicity will help you in all the trials of life. That which seems long to unsimple souls will to you seem short; what is to them an eternity will be for you but a moment. That which troubles, disconcerts, discourages,

[51] Prov. 10:9.

and disheartens them, making them bitter, irritable, and dissatisfied, will leave you calm and peaceful.[52]

Those lofty snow-crowned summits, distinguished by their dazzling whiteness from the mountain peaks they overshadow when the storm bursts and descends upon them, are no less near to heaven, no less firm and serene, than when bathed in the light of an azure sky. And so it is with those souls whom simplicity has raised to union with God. They overcome the trials of life by their matchless purity; in anguish, they retain their calm and peace, dwelling ever as close to God as in the happiest days.

Moreover, when the storm has passed, the sky above those snow peaks is clearer, the air more transparent, and the light more penetrating, making them more beautiful than before. And thus it is that simple souls, when tried by suffering, take on in God's sight a new and splendid beauty, a transparent purity hitherto unknown to them.

Simplicity will not keep you from suffering, but will so change your suffering that you will no longer recognize

---

[52] "Those souls which are simple preserve their peace amid disturbance and sorrow" (St. Vincent de Paul).

it. You will no longer suffer in the same way. You will no longer, as do worldly people, make an ideal of *not* suffering. You will no longer say triumphantly, "He died without suffering; he never knew He was dying," as though suffering were the only evil in the world. Your point of view will be more lofty. You will condemn and detest such suffering only as it is apart from God, which is against Him; the suffering of the "bad thief."[53] But you will be able to accept for yourself and those dear to you the "blessed suffering" when it pleases God to send it to you and in the measure He wills that you should bear it.

You will make use of it and transform it; or, better still, it will, when received in the spirit of simplicity, transform *you* and make you become like Jesus, by piercing your hands and feet, lacerating your body, covering your head with wounds, and opening and penetrating your heart. Thus accepted, suffering will lose all bitterness; it will become sweet.

Simplicity will transform your whole outlook by putting you in the right, whether in questions of joy or of sorrow. It will make you see clearly that your only real sorrow should be to offend God, to displease Him, to

[53] Cf. Luke 23:39.

sadden His heart; or that others should offend, dishonor, and forsake Him. All this is what will wring tears from your eyes, and, if you become sufficiently holy, will cause you a sort of perpetual anguish like that of our Lord.

Full of this thought, the Curé d'Ars[54] proclaimed himself the most wretched of men, complaining that he constantly lived among sinners and, from morning until night, heard of the affronts offered to God. "Sinners," he cried, "will cause the death of the sinner!"

How far removed you are from such feelings. Humble yourself at least for your lack of them, and be simple enough to understand and admire them.

Simplicity will detach you from many worldly joys that are useless even when not ridiculous or impious. It will show you the misery of those foolish people who place their happiness in riches, pleasure, flattery, success, and beauty.

Unfortunate worldlings! They claim that joy is their share, and on hearing their shrill peals of laughter, one might believe them. But no, it is but a fictitious mirth, which ill conceals the wounds, the anguish of a heart

---

[54] The Curé d'Ars, or St. John Vianney (1786-1859), patron saint of parish priests.

given over to evil and sin. Joy dwells only in the heart that is pure and the soul that is simple, and therein it overflows and is diffused as a balm on all the sorrows of this world.[55]

Those souls who are simple, the Gospel assures us, are happy even in the midst of their tears, finding therein the divine consolation.

Simplicity will transform all the duties of life for you. Duties of a serious nature will appear even more pressing, more sacred, and in the light of simplicity, you will accomplish them more eagerly. Simplicity will raise up and magnify all lesser duties, showing you in the smallest and most humble the sign of God's majesty. What a help it will prove to you!

Above all, it is the material things of life that tire you — those little ordinary duties, the minor details of everyday life, renewed with despairing monotony, that catch you as in a net and, in time, become so burdensome. There lies our greatest source of discouragement.

You feel that you were made for great things, you aspire to lofty flights, and here you are so low, in a poor

[55] This truth has been emphasized in a very beautiful book: *Vers la Joie*, by Lucie Félix-Faure Goyau.

little bark afloat upon a muddy pool, to which there is no outlet, and therefore you despair. But here, within reach, you have an easy means by which to free yourself, blossom forth, soar to the highest regions, and accomplish those great things for which you hunger and thirst. And this means is simplicity.

God is to be found in each tiny trifle, in each commonplace occupation, as He was beneath the swaddling clothes in the stable at Bethlehem. He is there, but for want of simplicity, you cannot see Him.

If you are simple, you will see God in this cloud of vulgar, material, everyday actions, as our Lady and St. Joseph saw Him in the manger; and because you see Him so, such actions will in your eyes become great and holy.

Yes, simplicity elevates the most material duties of life. The simple soul understands that "the Word became flesh only that the flesh might in turn become the Word." Simplicity has the marvelous power of making dust divine.

"Simplicity," writes St. Francis de Sales, "gives to all our actions their merit and their splendor, as the root gives to the flowers and leaves their life and beauty and to fruit its savor. Simplicity is like the ashes that fall from a fire and that preserve it."

Strength in Simplicity

Finally, be simple in all your works, whether apostolic, charitable, or devotional. To be simple is to do all for God. Some occupy themselves with charitable work purely from motives of ostentation. They seek to be conspicuous, to take the lead, to exercise a power that flatters their love of authority. Others seek but a pastime, a useful diversion for their loneliness, a consolation for their sorrows. Others see only the philanthropic and social side of all good works. All such are very far from that simplicity which the Gospel preaches. They do not soar like the dove, but crawl about like barnyard fowls; they confine themselves to earthly thoughts.

Again, others sincerely wish their neighbor well. They earnestly desire for him all that is for the good of his body and soul, for his welfare and salvation; they truly forget themselves. But in their ardor to serve others, they lose sight of God, or at best they consider souls more than they do God. They love souls more for themselves than for Him, and instead of God being first in their intentions, and the love of souls coming after, it is God who takes the second place. They see God only across the vision of souls, instead of seeing souls in God and through Him. Here is already a certain simplicity, but not enough; the intention is lacking in purity.

Finally, there are persons who truly seek God, but still not as they should. Instead of serving God according to His plan, they serve Him according to their own. They wish to impose upon Him their views, their line of action — themselves, in effect. Therefore their simplicity is imperfect.

In all good works, true simplicity consists in acting for God with absolute purity of intention, seeking before all and above all to please Him.

However interesting your neighbor may be in himself, he is interesting above all for God's sake. It is good to devote yourself to others for love of them, but it is a thousand times better to do so for the love of God, with the thought ever before you that while you work for them, you glorify God.

If you are simple, God will be first in your thoughts and your will as well as in your heart. All will proceed from God; all will be done by Him and for Him; all will revert to Him. The glory of God, the service and love of God: this is the aim of the simple soul. He must not let souls absorb him by even their most lofty and pressing needs, but must untiringly rectify his intentions and direct them toward God, seeing God always in souls and souls in God.

And he must not forget that the one way to glorify God, to serve Him and prove his love for Him, is to do His will — that is, to give himself in the measure that God asks, never trying to do more and always acting according to God's plan, and not his own.

Therefore, you to whom God has given a sublime mission, either apostolic or charitable, if you are beset by profane, egotistical, and evil thoughts, drive them from you, and put in their place intentions that are wholly pure and thoughts that are wholly divine. If the demon whispers to you that you are looked up to because of your good works, that you are more deserving than others, if he incites you to be domineering or self-complacent, if he hides from your eyes the glory of God, showing you only human, earthly aims, close your eyes and close your ears to these perfidious suggestions, rectify your will, and say, "O Lord, I desire no other aim in life than to do Thy work, no other guide than Thy will, and no other happiness than to procure Thy glory by laboring for the salvation of souls."

Chapter Nine

Let simplicity
transform all you do

Be simple, therefore, in making God your aim, tending toward Him as your last end, and making Him the object of all your activities. Be simple in leaning upon God as a means. Be simple so that you may be humble, so that you may learn to acknowledge that of yourself you can do nothing and that, left to your own resources, you would find it impossible to do any good thing, as our Lord declares, "Without me you can do nothing."[56]

Be simple also so that you may be confident, convinced that by leaning upon God, counting upon His grace, you will not be deceived and that "you can do all things in Him that strengtheneth you."[57]

Be simple, so that you may know your own nothingness, your wretchedness, and your sin.

[56] John 15:5.
[57] Phil. 4:13.

Be simple, so that you may contemplate the heart of God, its love, and its infinite goodness, and so that you may rest in His grace with most perfect confidence.

Be simple in the smallest things as well as in great ones, and even more so, for small things more often present themselves and are most pleasing to God.

"Thou hast wounded my heart," cries the Spouse in the Song of Songs. "Thou hast ravished my heart with one of thy eyes, and with one of thy hairs."[58] What is there more wonderful, more essential, or more important than an eye? And what is more worthless than a hair?

Be prepared to suffer, to bear heavy crosses. Stimulate your love to the point of martyrdom. Offer our Lord all that is dearest to you — even your eyes and your life, if need be. These "great things" will touch His Heart.

But do not neglect the lesser ones; offer Him all that is most ordinary in your life, your very food and rest, according to the word of the apostle.[59] His Heart will also be touched by these little things.

[58] Cant. 4:9 (RSV = Song of Sol. 4:9).
[59] Cf. 1 Cor. 10:31.

St. Catherine of Siena,[60] wrapped in the most sublime meditation, lost in ecstasy, counseling the great of the earth by the light of her wisdom and contemplation, enraptured the heart of her Celestial Spouse; but she pleased Him no less when, at her father's bidding, she devoted herself to the humblest of household duties and tranquilly continued her meditation in the midst of these lowly tasks. Seeing in her father the person of our Lord, in her mother the Blessed Virgin, in her brothers the Apostles, she joyfully submitted to whatever was asked of her.

It is right and good that you should devote yourself to great things, to important and excellent works; but practice for the love of God those little humble virtues which spring up like flowers at the foot of the Cross: the bearing of some slight misfortune, some passing infirmity, a vexation, a disappointment, an offense, a humiliation, certain tiresome occupations at home or abroad. As such occasions are ever recurring, what a treasure of spiritual riches you can amass if you know how to profit by them!

[60] St. Catherine of Siena (c. 1347-1380), Dominican tertiary.

Strength in Simplicity

Is it not clear that simplicity is what you most lack? Ah, if you were truly simple, simple in all things and at every turn, with God, with others, and with yourself; if you were indeed perfectly simple, what more would be wanting?

You are sensitive and affectionate. You admit it; you constantly prove it; you claim even to be excessively so, since you suffer thereby.

You have energy and willpower. You display it; you daily expend it unsparingly.

You are tender, tactful, and intelligent. It is one of your triumphs.

You have noble, generous aspirations. You are made up of self-sacrifice and abnegation.

With such excellent qualities, and such efficacious virtues, why is your life too often commonplace, empty, and useless, at times even odious, culpable, and scandalous? What is it that is wanting? I repeat, you are lacking in simplicity. You do not know how to direct your strengths and your qualities; you do not know how to make use of them. You let them all run to waste and perish because you are not simple.

Simplicity ennobles all things, directs all, and makes use of all for the glory of God.

Consider the dove: it is marvelously equipped to rise on high, to soar, to attain with ease to the loftiest, most distant regions. And for this there is but one thing needful: that it should spread its wings and then make use of them. You are the dove, and simplicity the all-powerful wings. Why not hasten to make use of them? Oh, spread your wings speedily; with bold and rapid flight, you will traverse incredible space and attain even to God Himself.

Chapter Ten

Direct all things to God

And now, after what we have said, who would not wish to become simple? But how can this be achieved?

You must first meditate upon this virtue, in order to understand its primary importance, its absolute necessity, and to arouse within yourself the most ardent desire to possess it at any cost.

Without this ardent desire and resolute will, all of your efforts will be in vain. Your endeavors and your inclinations will woefully fail before your egoism, vanity, selfishness, passions, and all the human motives that constantly influence you and that overthrow the edifice of your simplicity as fast as you build it up.

But once possessed of the calm and resolute will to attain simplicity, this is what you must do:

• First, *order your life* in general, your occupations taken as a whole, and your manner of action, in such a way as to make sure that all you may do will be in accordance with the will of God.

You should choose a rule of life in the spirit of obedience and with the approval of a prudent director. It should be sufficiently broad and yielding to fit the varying demands of your condition and to lend itself to the innumerable unforeseen circumstances that will constantly arise to change your plans, yet sufficiently firm and precise to exclude capriciousness and the self-will ever so ready to escape from all order and duty. Such a rule is the first condition and the indispensable means to lead you to purity of intention and, from there, to simplicity.

Only thus can you be certain of truly seeking God's good pleasure as the ultimate end of your actions and of your whole life.

• Next, every night before you go to sleep, *consider the occupations of the next day,* consider what changes or additions must be made in your general plan, and prepare for all, having God's will constantly before you as the absolute and unchanging rule of all that you do.

• In the morning, on waking, *offer to God all your thoughts, words, and acts of the day.* Promise that you wish to do all for His sake, His glory, His service, and His love, in union with the acts that our Lord Jesus Christ and our most Blessed Lady accomplished on earth, and which the Holy Spirit ever perpetuates in this world by means of the righteous.

Already this first offering, if not retracted, will communicate to all your actions an intention that we call *virtual*, and which will suffice to render them supernatural. Your soul will be placed in an interior disposition of simplicity, and as long as this state continues, your acts will receive therefrom the seal of holiness, which will make them particularly pleasing to God.

Then from time to time, especially when beginning each action, and particularly in the case of the longest and most important, remember to renew your morning resolution, if only by mentally saying, "O God, I do this for Thy sake. For love of Thee, I offer this meditation, this task, this repast, this visit, this good work, this suffering, this trial."

It is told of a pious hermit that he never began an action without pausing to direct his glance toward Heaven, and when asked the reason for this, he replied, "The better to make sure of my aim." As the sportsman takes aim for a moment before shooting, the more surely to reach his mark, so the hermit aimed at God so that he might be more certain to reach Him. Follow his example; aim always at God before acting by means of an upright intention.

If, after this, during the act in question, a human intention steals in to tempt you, an intention less worthy, or even quite worthless, let it neither disturb nor arrest you; but simply reply, as did the venerable John of Avila[61] to vanity — "You come too late; I've given all to God" — and continue to act.

If the thought that the world will see your good works distresses and frightens you, do not stop for that either. Recall to mind the words of the Gospel: "Let your light shine before men, that they may see your works, and glorify your

---

[61] St. John of Avila (1500-1569), Spanish mystic.

Father who is in Heaven."[62] The good that you do in the sight of the world may cause others to follow your example, and thus God will be glorified. Rejoice in this thought, and forget the praise and advantages that may fall to your share. And so your intention will remain pure.

• During your actions — above all, those of a certain duration — *renew your intention* by raising your heart to God, repeating, "For Thy sake, my God." Pause sometimes for an instant in the midst of a task, if it is possible without detriment to what you are doing, and say to yourself, "What is my object in this?" and therewith promptly reply, "Thou, my God, Thou alone!"

If you are disturbed in the midst of a meditation or a prayer; if, for reasons of health, you are kept from Mass or from your customary Communions, recall to mind that you must be ready "to leave God for God," and that, in thus giving up without irritation a pious devotion dear to your heart, you unite yourself still more closely to

---

[62] Matt. 5:16.

Him, you progress in simplicity and accordingly in perfection.

Beware of eagerness, precipitation, agitation, and irritability; beware of too natural an activity, sometimes feverish, which God does not bless.

Be calm, peaceful, and quiet, if not in the imagination and senses, and those inferior faculties of the soul which the will cannot always master, at least be so in that higher self, in those superior powers of the soul, in those lofty regions where God looks to judge you, and which alone are wholly governed by your free will. "Make haste slowly." You will find God more surely.

• *Make use of aspirations* — that is, brief, spontaneous prayers — as often as possible. In so doing, do not hesitate to use certain means that might appear childish if the end in view did not lend them an infinite dignity. Promise yourself, for instance, that when you hear the clock strike, when you pass from one room to another, when you sit down at table or at your desk, when you seal a letter or collect your things to go out, on entering a house or on leaving it, and in hundreds of other circumstances that you will determine, to raise your heart for an instant to God. No means are petty when used for great ends.

In proportion as you make it a habit to have recourse to God, your heart will expand and your love will increase. Soon you will no longer have need of such methods and means. Your soul will so hunger and thirst for God, that you will, of yourself, unceasingly turn to Him.

The needle of a compass points north; if you turn it aside, it weighs against your finger, showing its natural tendency and, from the moment all pressure ceases, returns to its original direction. And so the person who has become truly simple turns continually to God, impelled by an instinctive need. If apparently turned aside by the duties of life, he always tends to return to Him, and as soon as he can, he does so completely.

Chapter Eleven

*Find simplicity
in attentiveness to
God's presence*

A last means of acquiring simplicity — and the best — is the practice of the presence of God. It is of such importance that I must lay great stress upon it. As simplicity is the foundation of perfection, so the sense of the presence of God is the foundation of simplicity. Simplicity, in fact, consists in acting for God; it is therefore plain that before all you must think of God, and this you will never do better than if you are always conscious of His presence.

Let us further explain this influence of the sense of the presence of God upon simplicity. The sense of the presence of God will make you simple for two reasons:

• In the presence of God, all evil intentions become impossible.

• God's presence will efficaciously stimulate the purest of intentions.

In the first place, the sense of the presence of God will put to flight all evil intentions, will destroy the "lust of the eye,"[63] and will preserve you from sin. It is because the sinner forgets that he is seen by God, says the psalmist, that he sins so continually.[64] And after having enumerated at length the crimes of Jerusalem, the prophet Ezekiel finally reproaches her with forgetfulness of God as the cause of all her disorders.

How often priests find proof of this in the confessional. When after long and painful avowals they say to a penitent, "In the midst of your sins, had you no thought of God?" the reply often is, "No, Father, I had forgotten Him"; or, "The thought of Him was too painful, so I put it from me"; or sometimes again, "It was the thought of Him that brought me back."

A sinner flees from the presence of God to escape the remorse of conscience. When Adam sinned, he hid himself, no longer able to bear the sight of his Creator. And when called, he paid no heed; twice God had to call him and summon him to appear before Him.[65] And

---

[63] 1 John 2:16.

[64] Cf. Ps. 9b:5 (RSV = Ps. 10:4).

[65] Cf. Gen. 3:8-10.

so it is with children: they hide while doing wrong, and when it is done, they try to escape all notice. The mere sight of you stops them, troubles them; they are afraid.

If the thought of his parents, the sight of them, and the fear of their punishments, serve to arrest a child, how much more will the thought and fear of God exercise upon us an all-powerful influence!

"All sins," says St. Teresa, "are committed because we do not think of God as really present, but imagine Him as very far away." If we said to ourselves, "God is here. God sees me. God judges me. In a single instant, God could bring my life to an end and cast me into eternal darkness," then fear would triumph over pleasure, satisfaction, and temptation; and even if, taken unawares, our weakness should cause our downfall, we could not remain in a state of sin.

If we said to ourselves, "God is here, and I am outraging Him. God loads me with favors, and I am overwhelming Him with contempt. God died for me, and I am crucifying Him once more," then truly love would fill our hearts — an all-powerful, infinite love wherein to find strength to rise triumphant over all difficulties.

"If," says St. Thomas, "we always remembered that God is present and that He sees all, we would never or almost never commit a sin." And St. Jerome[66] expresses the same idea, saying, "The thought of God closes the door upon all sin."

St. Ambrose[67] relates that during a solemn sacrifice offered to the gods by Alexander the Great, a young page carried a lighted torch by the side of his sovereign. In the course of the ceremony, the flame reached the child's hand, and although he could have saved himself by letting the torch fall, he bore without flinching the frightful pain, fearing his master's displeasure. "Respect for the royal majesty," cried St. Ambrose, "could even in a feeble child so triumph over nature." How much more surely should respect for the Divine Majesty impel a Christian soul to overcome all temptations and to endure all ills rather than offend God to His face.

"If we were careful to keep ourselves in God's presence," says St. John Chrysostom,[68] "we would never think, say, or do any wrong thing, for we would say to ourselves unceasingly: God sees all; God beholds all my actions."

---

[66] St. Jerome (c. 342-420), biblical scholar.

[67] St. Ambrose (c. 339-397), Bishop of Milan.

[68] St. John Chrysostom (c. 347-407) Bishop of Constantinople; called "Golden Mouth" for his eloquence.

The practice of the presence of God is thus a sovereign remedy against sin, because it makes all guilty intentions impossible. Beneath the eye of God, the heart is purified; all unworthy sentiments become unbearable; all that is contrary to simplicity is destroyed and, as one might say, "consumed by the divine fire."

Soldiers become as it were electrified beneath the eye of their leader, be he an Alexander, a Charlemagne, or a Napoleon, and, so inspired, they fly joyfully to meet danger and shed their blood for their country. Shall the eye of the sovereign Master of Heaven and earth, the eye of God Himself, have less power over our hearts?

In the springtime, under the fresh warm light of the sun, the earth renews its youth. All nature was dead, but beneath the kindly touch of the sun's sweet rays, life flows afresh, and the whole world of nature — trees, leaves, and flowers — blossoms forth anew.

Is not God the sun of the world, the sun of souls? Beneath His divine glance and in His divine presence, the most callous and indifferent souls will receive new life; the Christian life will flow anew, lofty desires will blossom, and all the virtues will bloom. The presence of God is all powerful in impelling us toward good, all powerful in increasing our love and leading us onward toward perfection. This is what God taught Abram when he said, "Walk before me, and be perfect."[69]

Perfection is love. But how can the love of God take shape without the thought of God? And on the other hand, with the thought of Him, how can this love fail to increase? Even human friendships are strengthened by frequent interchanges, and yet, but for rare and noble exceptions, it is the faults and failings rather than the good qualities that we mutually discover as friendship develops. But with God, the more you know Him, the more you will think of Him, and the more you will reflect on the remembrance of His graces and His love, His greatness and His favors; the more, also, you will be drawn toward Him by a gentle, irresistible power. Between Him and you, between God and your soul, by the habit of placing yourself before Him and of living in His presence, there will be formed a tender and intimate union that each day will strengthen.

Prayers, meditations, reading, and pious exercises will not suffice for this growth of love. "While on the fire, water boils," says St. John Chrysostom, "but when removed, it soon grows cold." To keep love from growing

[69] Gen. 17:1.

cold, you must think of the presence of God. Often renew in your heart acts of fervor, and unceasingly keep your soul turned toward Heaven as the sunflower turns its face toward the sun.

"When you love," says St. Teresa, "you unceasingly think of the beloved one, and so your love grows greater." The thought of God will increase your love and make you rapidly advance in the path of perfection, for it will soon lead you to simplicity.

Chapter Twelve

*Learn the ways
to be attentive to
God's presence*

As we have said, the habitual sense of the presence of God is thus the essential foundation of simplicity. But how can we form this precious habit? By removing the obstacles and by taking certain measures.

First, remove the obstacles. These include dissipation of mind and attachment to trifles, futilities, things of no importance; lack of reflection, the habit of letting thoughts and imagination wander without guidance or control; foolish reading, frivolous company, and endless conversations that are perfectly useless. The obstacles are also to be found in an unruly heart, in the outward distractions on which it is set; in certain unfortunate, even dangerous, friendships; in engrossing affections, violent passions, eager desires, and too hastily formed resolutions. And, finally, obstacles are found in the examples of the world, with its unprofitable amusements; the frittering away of life, leaving you no longer master of yourself; and in an undisciplined life, made up of whims and fancies.

You must get rid of all this, control your thoughts and affections, and direct your whole life, for this is the required condition preparatory to all serious thought of God.

Next, take positive measures; make use of your intelligence and your affections and will, the former to consider the fact of God's presence, the latter to unite yourself to Him by acts of love and desire.

The exercise of the intelligence is the easier of the two. God is everywhere present; faith teaches us this: "All the earth is filled with His glory."[70] "God is mindful," says St. Augustine, "of each one of your thoughts, words, and actions, as though you were the only creature in the world, and you alone wholly occupied the divine consciousness." And he further represents the creature with regard to God as a sponge immersed in the ocean. God is immense, and the creature is, in a way, lost in Him.

God sees all things at one moment of time; all is observed and remembered by Him. On the Day of

[70] Cf. Ps. 71:19 (RSV = Ps. 72:19).

Judgment, He will recall all things to us: "Then shall you behold a book," the Church tells us, "wherein all these things are written."[71]

Not only is God present to all creatures, but He acts in all; they have strength and life and are capable of action and expression only because of Him. "He is in the sun," says St. Liguori, "to give us light, in fire to give us heat, in water to refresh us, in bread to nourish us, in clothing to cover us, and in all things for our service."

This wondrous thought has caused the very saints to tremble with emotion. When St. Francis of Assisi[72] contemplated nature, he was lost in ecstasy. He would pause to call to the birds, to bid them sing the praises of God.

"O God!" exclaimed St. Augustine, in a transport of love, "Heaven and earth and all creation call upon me to love You"; and casting his eyes upon the sea, the mountains, and the plains, raising them even to the starry skies, he felt that all things found voice to cry, "Augustine, love God, for He created thee only to be loved by thee."

---

[71] *Dies Irae*, strophe 5.

[72] St. Francis of Assisi (c. 1182-1226), founder of the Franciscan Order.

St. Mary Magdalene de' Pazzi, filled with love and admiration at the sight of a beautiful flower, sighed in rapture, "From all eternity, God thought of creating this flower for me."

Others, like St. Teresa, when considering the marvelous works of God, have heard, as it were, a universal chorus, reproaching them with their ingratitude toward their Creator.

St. Simeon Salus[73] would strike with his staff the flowers of the fields and the grass of the meadows, saying, "Hush! God has made you so beautiful for love of me that I might learn to love Him; but, alas, I love Him not. Oh, hush, then, and cease to reproach me with my ingratitude! I can longer bear your reproof."

Follow, then, the example of the saints. Behold God in nature, God present everywhere. But, above all, behold God in His masterpieces, in reasoning creatures; behold Him in yourself. "Know you not," said St. Paul, "that you are the temple of God, and that the Spirit of God dwelleth in you?"[74] and he often reverted to this

[73] St. Simeon Salus, sixth-century Egyptian who spent twenty-nine years of penitential life in the desert.

[74] 1 Cor. 3:16.

thought, such was the importance he attached to it. And this was because he understood the teaching of the divine Master: "If anyone loves me . . . my Father will love him, and we will come to him and will make our abode with him."[75]

God dwells in the soul of the righteous person. He makes it His permanent abode, His royal residence. To find God, you have only to retire within yourself in perfect recollection.

When St. Catherine of Siena was prevented by her parents from going to church, she withdrew, she tells us, into the little sanctuary she had made within herself, and there, amid her overburdening duties, she continued in perfect recollection her loving conversation with God.

A last exercise is to apply your intelligence to Jesus Christ, in thinking of the Savior and in calling to mind the various phases of His existence: at Bethlehem, in the desert, at Nazareth, during his public life, in His Passion, on Calvary, in the tomb, or risen and ascended in Heaven at the right hand of His Father. But this exercise of your intelligence does not suffice; your will and

[75] John 14:23.

affections must be brought into play by the acts you will make.

Think of God as present and active, God who sees, hears, and judges you, and make acts of faith, adoration, submission, supplication, love, and total self-sacrifice. And, above all, in thinking of Jesus Christ, make frequent acts of love, acts that come from the very depths of your heart, by which, in a way, you place your heart wholly in His.

May Jesus Christ become your Friend in the full meaning of the word — the true and faithful Friend of whom Holy Scripture speaks, saying, "He is a protection and a strong defense, a very refuge in life and in eternity";[76] and of whom the *Imitation* further says, "Without this Friend, thou canst not well live, [for] he that cleaveth unto creatures shall fall with that which is subject to fall, but he that embraceth Jesus shall stand forever."[77]

May Jesus be your Friend in all afflictions of heart, soul, and mind; in trials, sadness, or neglect.

---

[76] Cf. Ecclus. 6:14, 16 (RSV = Sir. 6:14, 16).

[77] Thomas à Kempis (c. 1380-1471; ascetical writer), *Imitation of Christ*, Bk. 2, ch. 8.

At times, your heart aches from its very fullness, and you must confide in someone to find relief from this oppression. And yet when you seek this necessary consolation in a creature, how often you find but an illusion, how rarely the reality!

But who, on the other hand, ever turned to Jesus without receiving the most marvelous help? Since Mary Magdalene bared her heart to Him, as with her tears she bathed His feet,[78] what broken heart weeping near the Savior has ever failed to find unhoped-for strength together with all loving consolation? "At the thought of God," cried David, "my heart was filled with joy and consolation."[79]

When a Christian can say, "Jesus suffered and died for me. He has already borne my sorrows and sufferings, and borne them to merit grace and strength for me. When He hung upon the Cross, He thought of me, He saw me, and even now from the height of Heaven, He is looking down upon me, thinking of me, and praying for me," what more could he ask? Jesus is the divine Friend who consoles and strengthens, the Friend who revives

[78] Luke 7:37 ff.
[79] Cf. Ps. 15:8-9 (RSV = Ps. 16:8-9).

us in our moments of weakness and sustains us in the hour of temptation.

If you are tempted, remember that He was tried before you. If you are governed by pride, self-love, or vanity, think of Jesus during His Passion, covered with blows, spat upon, humiliated, and crowned with thorns.

If you are beset by laziness and sensuality, think of Jesus covered with a bloody sweat, scourged, carrying His Cross; think of Him hanging upon it, His hands and feet pierced, His sacred body torn, devoured by thirst and shattered by pain.

If you are a slave to material things, think of Jesus poor and wholly destitute at Bethlehem, at Nazareth, and during His public life; think of Him upon the Cross, rendering His soul in the supreme embrace of poverty.

If you fall into sin, remember that Jesus fell three times on the road to Calvary so that He might merit for you the grace to rise again after your falls as He rose after His, and so that discouragement might never enter your heart.

And if at times the trials and the burden of life are too heavy, if nature rebels and, in spite of yourself, you cry out, "I can bear no more," remember that Jesus in His human nature knew this extremity, the very brink of despair, and that He, too, cried out: "My Father . . . let this chalice pass from me! My God, my God, why hast Thou forsaken me?"[80]

Jesus is furthermore the Friend who counsels, inspires, and directs us. In all matters of initiative, in necessary decisions, in the forming of plans, the accepting of responsibilities, in the advice you give, and in the influence you have over those entrusted to you, He will help, enlighten, and lead you. He will prompt the word to be spoken, the counsel to be given, the measure to be taken. He will relieve all anxiety and anguish. He will give you peace and tranquillity concerning the decisions you have made.

Jesus is the Friend who will help you in prayer, who will fix your attention, keep your thoughts from wandering, and attach your mind and heart to His Father, for no one goes to His Father save by Him.[81] He is the Way, the Door that leads to His Father's house. Without Him, your prayers will be only vain words, powerless to rise above earth; with Him, they become living holy voices that will rise as high as Heaven and reach the ear of God.

---

[80] Matt. 26:39, 27:46.
[81] Cf. John 14:6.

Strength in Simplicity

May Jesus be for you the Friend of each hour. Think, speak, act, and rest in union with Him, and I make bold to say with St. Paul, eat and drink with Him, and, like Him, for the glory of His Father.[82] When you awake, call upon Jesus. Call upon Him at the beginning and end of each action. Pause from time to time to cast a glance toward Him, as a mother interrupts her work, her very breathing, to glance toward the child who plays or works by her side. Call upon Jesus when you are leaving home and upon your return. Call upon Him a last time before you fall asleep.

Make Jesus the beginning, the center, and the end of all things. May His name always be for you first and last, your *alpha* and *omega*. May Jesus have the first place, the place of honor, the royal place, in your heart.

In the world, we see silly, frivolous people, vain, material creatures, who think only of the world's opinion. This thought absorbs and guides them; they are possessed, hypnotized, by it. On rising, while dressing, when at table, at home or abroad, in their thoughts, words, or actions, always and everywhere, they ask themselves, "What will the world say?" For them, the world is a real

[82] Cf. 1 Cor. 10:31.

and perpetual presence, an ever-watchful eye, by which they are governed, conquered, and enslaved. May Jesus be to you what the world is to them, and may your whole life be inspired by the desire to please Him.

Today the world expels Jesus from its midst. Today men cry as did those before them, "We will not have Him to reign over us; take Him away and crucify Him!"[83] "The nations have trembled," says the psalmist. "All the powers of the earth have gathered together against the Lord and against His Christ."[84] It is a conspiracy that savors of madness; they would abolish the very name of God.

It is for you to make amends by quietly protesting and resisting as a Christian may. It is for you to give your heart to Jesus all the more generously as the world gives Him less, and to receive Him with all the more love in proportion as others drive Him away with a more intense hatred.

Live beneath the eye of God, united to Jesus in thought and will, in heart and soul. Make Him known. Manifest Him to those around you. Be, as it were, a

[83] Cf. John 19:15.
[84] Cf. Ps. 2:2.

living mirror wherein His reflection may be seen, and let Him shine forth through your Christian influence upon all who approach you. In short, by means of simplicity and purity of intention, endeavor each day to grow in the true and pure love of Jesus for His own sake.

The simpler you are, the more closely will you be united to Jesus; and as you are more closely united to Him, so will you become simpler. Thus is formed a double current that will bear you to the highest point of perfection. By means of simplicity, like the Apostles on Mount Tabor, you will "see no one, but Jesus only."[85] The more clearly you see Him, the more you will love Him; and in proportion as you become united to Him, just so fully will you become the living manifestation of His supreme prayer: "That they all may be one, as Thou, Father, in me, and I in Thee: that they also may be one in us."[86]

God will help you in this great work, this marvelous work of holiness, a work that is His even more than yours.

[85] Matt. 17:8.
[86] John 17:21.

God loves your soul more than the most loving mother ever loved her children, more than the most tender and devoted wife ever loved her husband. God loves your soul with an incomprehensible love, because He is infinite. And because He so loves your soul, He unceasingly urges it to the conquest of that most precious of virtues — namely, simplicity.

It is because God loves your soul that He wills to fashion it Himself. And if He wills to ennoble and beautify it, if He desires to bless it and overwhelm it with favors, He will send you vexatious disappointments and failures, opposition and mortifications, so that you may not attach yourself to creatures, but solely to Him. He will cause you to fail where you hoped to succeed, and He will use means unthought of by you to ensure final success. He will contrive to show you your own nothingness, to prove to you that in the work of your sanctification, all that is lasting will be done by Him alone.

On the ruins of self, He will raise up the edifice of your perfection. He may even divest you of all things, and perhaps, at moments, He will let you believe that He Himself has abandoned you, in order to make you become more like unto Jesus uttering His cry of distress and desolation.[87] But it is just then that He will be nearest to you, will most effectively sustain you, and be most truly present within you. He will use these trials as marvelous remedies to free you from your imperfections and to open your eyes more and more fully to the uncreated beauty and splendor of the supernatural world.

Thenceforward you will become more like the elect in Heaven. By means of simplicity, God will become all in all to you as He is to them, while awaiting the day when, freed from the encumbrance of the flesh, you will rise to contemplate Him face-to-face and to know Him forever as you are known to Him.

Then your simplicity will be perfect, because there can never be anything further to separate you from God, and you will live forever enraptured in the sight of the divine beauty and in the unutterable enjoyment and perfect possession of the "one thing necessary."[88] Here below, all are not called to the same degree of simplicity, but you should desire this most admirable virtue. Seek it out, and practice it in the measure that God wills and in proportion to the grace that He gives you,

[87] Cf. Matt. 27:46.
[88] Luke 10:42.

Learn the ways to be attentive

for simplicity is your greatest treasure in this world, as it will be your highest reward in the next. In the measure that you have been simple on earth you will be glorified in Heaven.